ALGEBRA & GEOMETRY

KINGFISHER

NEW YORK

KINGFISHER
LONDON & NEW YORK

Consultant: Dr. Troy P. Regis

Designed and created by Basher www.basherbooks.com
Text written by Dan Green

Dedicated to Bill Penn and the Elephant Boys

Distributed in the U.S. by Macmillan,
175 Fifth Ave., New York, NY 10010

Library of Congress Cataloging-in-Publication
data has been applied for.

ISBN: 978-0-7534-6597-4

Kingfisher books are available for special promotions and premiums.
For details contact: Special Markets Department, Macmillan,
175 Fifth Avenue, New York, NY 10010.

For more information, please visit www.kingfisherbooks.com

Printed in China
9 8 7 6 5 4 3 2 1
1TR/0411/WKT/UNTD/140MA

CONTENTS

Introduction
Algebra and Geometry

Math is all around you. There are treasures to count up and cakes to divide. You'll find number sequences in a sunflower's delicate spirals, in the honeycombs of busy bees, and—watch out!—in the rapid spread of deadly bacteria. But hey, no matter what happens in *this* crazy, chaotic world, in peaceful Mathland, two plus one is *always* three. Oh yeah, there's safety in numbers.

Pythagoras was an ancient Greek who loved to give his brain a good workout. Geometry kept his mind fit! He found out amazing stuff about numbers and shapes— most famously, his theorem on triangles. Algebra, with its *a*'s, *b*'s, and *x*'s, is simply a method of doing math when you don't have all the facts at hand—kind of like detective work. Pythagoras understood that, although math is counting and business and real-world things, it also exists in a world of its own. This means that you can share ideas with anyone, no matter what language they speak. Even aliens! If extraterrestrials are smart enough to build a spaceship, chances are they'll also know how to count! Get ready to take things to the next level.

Pythagoras

CHAPTER 1
Counting Crew

Meet the gang who got this adventure started. And let's begin with the amazing idea that a written symbol can stand in for something you can count. That's right! The Counting Crew began as scratches in stones or collections of sticks that somehow represented numbers. They've been around for a while, and they're smart fellows, too. You read numbers from left to right, like words, but you can tell the value of a number by working your way from right to left. The place value increases with each digit, to give you ones, tens, hundreds, and so on. Make no mistake—these dudes are the math symbols that count!

Roman
Numerals

Arabic
Numerals

Zero

Unity

Negative
Number

Base 2

Base 10

Significant
Figure

Roman Numerals

■ Counting Crew

☀ Numerals are symbols that are used to represent numbers
☀ This number system is fiendishly difficult to handle
☀ There is no Roman numeral for zero

I'm an ancient numbering system, dating back to the days when men wore skirts and sandals. I use capital letters for numbers: I = 1; V = 5; X = 10; L = 50; C = 100; D = 500; M = 1,000. Reading from the left, III = 3, VII = 7, and XX = 20. But 4 is not IIII, it's IV! That's because a smaller value numeral *in front* of a large one tells you to subtract! So, IX = 9 and XL = 40. It makes me a nightmare to do math problems with!

Roman Numerals

● Earliest known use: around 9 B.C.
● 1 to 10 in Roman numerals: I, II, III, IV, V, VI, VII, VIII, IX, X
● Commonly used for clocks, copyrights, and the Super Bowl

Arabic Numerals

Counting Crew

* Official international number system and language of math
* Properly called Hindu-Arabic numerals
* First system to acknowledge zero as a number

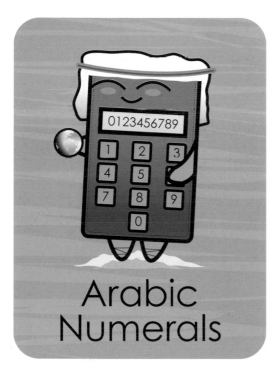

Arabic Numerals

With roots in ancient Indian and Arabian trade and mathematics, I'm used all over the world for measuring and counting. You know me—I'm the system of ten numbers you learned at school: 0, 1, 2, 3, 4, 5, 6, 7, 8, and 9. Each number has its own value, plus another value given by its position. Take 794: this means seven hundreds (7 x 100), nine tens (9 x 10), and four ones (4 x 1). Sure beats DCCXCIV*!

* Earliest known use: A.D. 500
* Multiples of 9 (18, 45, 198) also have digits that add up to a multiple of 9
* *DCCXCIV: the equivalent of 794 in Roman numerals

Zero
■ Counting Crew

☀ The number with the hole in the middle, AKA nil or naught
☀ This goose-egg digit helps make huge or tiny numbers
☀ The first even digit of the set of whole numbers

Think I'm nothin'? Think I ain't somethin'? Mr. Unity acts like he's the Big Cheese, like he's the only one with any value. Well, I may be *worth* nothin', but I *mean* a lot. Just let me loose with my friends, Arabic Numerals and Base 10, and you'll see all kinds of math mastery.

After 9 comes 10: it's me that signals a change of place value from ones to tens (in this case), or tens to hundreds, and so on. When I follow a number, I make it ten times bigger—2 becomes 20, then 200, then 2,000. Add me to a number and nothing happens, but subtract a number from *me* and you'll dive into Negative Number's murky depths. Multiply a number by me, and I make it disappear. Ask me to divide, though, and I'll create mathematical mayhem. Man, I've got zero tolerance for that!

● First recorded use: A.D. 458
● $x^0 = 1$ (in other words, any number to the power of zero = 1)
● Googol: 1 followed by one hundred zeros

Zero

Unity
■ Counting Crew

☀ This special one is the number between 0 and 2
☀ The first positive odd number
☀ In probability, 1 is a 100% likely chance—a certainty

I am your Number One, the top of the pile, the king of math mountain. Tall and slender, I'm what every number longs to be. I'm the first nonzero whole number.

My math wizardry is simply beguiling. Just think of the biggest number you can and then add 1. See? Adding me to any number makes it bigger and bigger and bigger—ever closer to infinity. I'm not a composite number, nor am I a prime number. I can change Odd Number into Even Number and Even into Odd. Integers (whole numbers) are always divisible by me. And I'm unique in that any number multiplied by me is still itself—even me: I am my own square, my own cube, my own fourth power, and so on (1 x 1 = 1; 1 x 1 x 1 = 1). I'm the only *one* who can say this, and my Unity comes from being so pure. It's mystifying!

● Factor: a number by which a larger number can be divided equally
● Prime number: has only two factors (1 and itself—e.g., 13)
● Composite number: has more than two factors—e.g., 12 (factors: 1, 2, 3, 4, 6, 12)

Unity

13

Negative Number

■ Counting Crew

✳ Natural numbers are those above zero, used for counting
✳ This *unnatural* critter is lower in value than zero
✳ Always starts with a minus sign

They say I'm not natural and that I bring the number world down. It's just not fair. They make me wear a minus sign (–), and that's a real downer, too. Okay, okay, I know I've got negative vibes, but you'd have them, too, if you had to live in this chilly, subzero zone. It's *brrr*, no doubt!

I'm what happens if you try to subtract a bigger number from a smaller one. It's something you can't do in the real world (just try to take nine candies from a bag that has only five in it). In mind-bending Mathland, however, nothing could be easier. You think Arabic Numerals stop at Zero? No sir! They get to Zero and just keep going— *backward*: 0, –1, –2, –3. Take nine from six and you get minus three; add three to minus three and you get zero. You're right, there's nothing natural in that!

● A negative number x a positive number = a negative number
● A negative number ÷ a positive number = a negative number
● A negative number x or ÷ a negative number = a positive number

Negative Number

Base 2
■ Counting Crew

☀ "Base" simply means how far you count before repeating
☀ Computers do their calculations using base 2
☀ Also known as the binary system

I work with two numbers—0 and 1—and each place value *doubles* as you work to the left. So, the last number on the right counts ones, the next to the left counts twos, then fours, then eights, and so on. With me? C'mon, it's easy: 10 in base 2 (10_2) equals 2. That's because the 0 means no ones and the 1 means one two. It's pretty "base"-ic, really. You try, with 10011_2*.

Base 2

● First known use: around 100 B.C. (India)
● Numbers 1 to 10 in base 2: 1, 10, 11, 100, 101, 110, 111, 1000, 1001, 1010
● *10011_2 = (1 x 16) + (0 x 8) + (0 x 4) + (1 x 2) + (1 x 1) = 19

Base 10
Counting Crew ■

* System that counts in sets of ten, tallying ones, tens, hundreds
* A natural way of counting that uses the tips of your ten digits
* Also known as the decimal system

Base 10

When it comes to getting somewhere with numbers, you can sure *count* on me to help. I work in sets of ten, where each place is ten times the value of the one to its right. It might sound tricky, but really it isn't. See, 39 means three tens and nine ones. The position containing the 3 (tens) is worth ten times the position containing the 9 (ones). Now that's gotta be worth some at-"ten"-tion!

● First known use: around 540 B.C. (China)
● Also referred to as powers of 10: $1{,}093 = (1 \times 10^3) + (0 \times 10^2) + (9 \times 10^1) + (3 \times 10^0)$
● *Digit* comes from the Latin word for finger (*digitus*)

Significant Figure

Counting Crew

- ✳ This confident dude helps tidy up unnecessary extra digits
- ✳ Shortened to sig. fig. or s.f., for ease of use
- ✳ Not to be confused with decimal place

I'm your straight-dealing, no-nonsense kind of operator, sifting out unhelpful information to give you useful, relevant numbers. I help exercise a little control!

If I told you that 5,200 people attended a gig, would you think that exactly 5,200 came? No! You'd know this was an estimate given to the nearest hundred. This calculation is up to me and written using sig. figs.* The *precise* number of people may not be known or relevant, so I round up or down to tell you *roughly* how many people came, while still being accurate enough to use! (The actual number is between 5,100 and 5,300, since I have two sig. figs.) My rules are simple: the first nonzero digit in a number is the first sig. fig.; the second is the next and so on. This means that 0.005108 has the same number of sig. figs. as 3,007 (four).

- ● To find a sig. fig., use the next digit for rounding up or down: 4.067 = 4.07 (3 s.f.)
- ● Round up with a next digit of 5 or over, otherwise round down: 4.064 = 4.06 (3 s.f.)
- ● *5,183 people attended the gig, so 5,200 has been rounded up to two sig. figs.

Significant Figure

CHAPTER 2
Number Nuts

Meet the Number Nuts—a *prime* bunch, indeed! Here, you've got solid, dependable Integer, equitable Even, and reasonable Rational Number. Look closer and you'll also find quirky and radical Odd, Irrational, and Imaginary numbers among their ranks. And lurking between them all are those bit players, Fraction and Decimal. Underestimate this crew at your peril! It's bursting at the seams—count up from Zero and you'll see that there are gazillions of them. You can't even list all the numbers from 0 to 1—there's 0.1, but also 0.11 and 0.111 and 0.1111 and . . . feeling number nutty? Don't let these guys do a number on you!

Integer

Even Number

Odd Number

Prime Number

Power

Fraction

Decimal

Rational Number

Irrational Number

Imaginary Number

Integer

■ Number Nuts

✸ All whole numbers, including zero, are integers
✸ Can be positive or negative (excluding zero)
✸ You round a decimal number up (or down) to make it whole

Well rounded and complete, I have it organized. The full-fat digit with no messy fractions or trailing decimal parts, I am your bona-fide whole number.

I've got my feet firmly on the ground, helping you count real-life things—stuff like ice-cream cones, friends, and skateboards. Say, when did you last hear of half a telephone or 4.3 trucks? Exactly! You simply can't get enough of my wholesome goodness. My pals and I go into infinity, and some of us even claim to be perfect! Oh yeah, a perfect number is very special, indeed. Its proper factors add up to its total. Take the number 6, for example: its proper factors are 1, 2, and 3. Add these up and you get 6. Completely useless, but utterly satisfying! See if you can find the next one*.

● Proper factors: the numbers by which a figure can be divided, excluding itself
● Z: the set of all integers where, for example, Z_{10} is the set of integers from 1 to 9
● *Next perfect number: 28 (1 + 2 + 4 + 7 + 14)

Integer

23

Even Number

Number Nuts

✳ Any integer that ends in 0, 2, 4, 6, or 8
✳ Can always be divided into two equal parts
✳ All known perfect numbers are even and end in 6 or 8

Hey there. I'm Mr. Trustworthy, the honest guy, the good cop. You can always count on me to play it by the book. Unlike elusive Prime Number and quirky Odd, I am easy to work with. Even-steven, that's me.

I like to keep things nice and neat. Chop me into two exact same halves and I guarantee you'll never find any remainders—not a single one! Oh no, I always finish up my plate; no leftovers here. Makes perfect sense, doesn't it? Because I'm easy to split into equal parts, you'll never have any trouble finding some of my factors. Those are the numbers that will divide me exactly. (One of them will always be 2, for a start.) You see, I'm not very tricky and I don't try to get you in trouble or rock the boat. Life is so much easier when you stay on an *even* keel!

● Adding two even numbers together = an even number
● Adding two odd numbers together = an even number
● Any two even numbers multiplied together = an even number

Even Number

Odd Number

Number Nuts

* Any integer that ends in 1, 3, 5, 7, or 9
* Can't be divided into two equal parts without a remainder
* No known perfect numbers are odd

I'm a funny one—the odd bod who simply refuses to be divided by two without there being something left over. Take the number 7, for example: 7 divided by 2 equals 3 . . . plus 1; okay, um, 23 divided by 2 equals 11 . . . mmm, plus 1 again. That's odd, you might say, there's always a one left over, a remainder. But that's just how I operate: that's me.

And where would you be without me? You see, Even Number counts up in steps of two, but what happens in between? Well, that's where things start to get interesting. I fill in the gaps to give you three's company, the fifth element, seventh heaven, and unlucky (for some) thirteen. Want to know what makes me a real oddity, though? Try taking one odd number from another—say 5 from 11. I know! It's even! Now that really *is* odd.

● Adding two odd numbers together = an even number
● Subtracting one odd number from another = an even number
● Any two odd numbers multiplied together = an odd number

Odd Number

Prime Number
Number Nuts

✻ A number that can be divided evenly *only* by 1 and itself
✻ A positive integer that is not a prime is a composite number
✻ 1 is not a prime number because it only has one divisor (1)

I am one prime cut! Built like a football lineman, I'm the beefcake of the Number Nutters and a nice meaty subject to get your teeth into, believe me.

To join my club, a number must have just two divisors. Try to find factors for one of my gang—say, 13: 6 x 2 = 12 (too low) and 7 x 2 = 14 (too high). The only combination of numbers multiplied together that will give you 13 is 1 x 13. So, now you know I'm exclusive, but did you know that I'm also elusive? Oh yeah, finding new primes is a favorite brain-busting activity for math geeks. There are an infinite number, but no one has developed a foolproof method for finding them. The largest known Prime to date contains almost 13 million digits—enough to fill more than 500 Basher books! I'm in my *prime*, I can tell you!

● First eleven prime numbers: 2, 3, 5, 7, 11, 13, 17, 19, 23, 29, 31
● Only even prime number: 2
● Magic prime: 73,939,133 (makes a new prime with each digit taken from the end)

Prime Number

Power

★ A handy method of repeat multiplication
★ Also known as exponentiation
★ Deals in massive numbers but also extremely teeny ones

I'm mathematical dynamite! I'm marked out by my exponent, which is written above and to the right of a number. I'm only small, but boy do I pack a punch—fire me up and I'll be belting out big numbers in no time.

My job is to multiply a number by itself again and again. Take small number 5, for example: 5^2 (five to the power of two, or five squared) means 5 x 5, which is 25; but 5^3 = 5 x 5 x 5 = 125; and 5^4 = 5 x 5 x 5 x 5 = 625. See how quickly I reach eye-wateringly vast extremes! And I work both ways—if my exponent is a negative number, I get exceedingly tiny (although I never drop below zero). For example 10^{-5} is 0.00001. You'll find me all over the place, especially in science, where I offer a neat way to write down huge and tiny numbers. Powerful stuff!

● Any number raised to the power of 1 is the number itself: 3^1 is the same as 1 x 3
● Smallest 5th power other than 1: 32 (2^5 or 2 x 2 x 2 x 2 x 2)
● Googolplex: 10^{googol} or 1 followed by 10^{100} zeros

Power

Fraction
Number Nuts

✳ This broken figure is more than zero but less than one
✳ Written as a numerator over a denominator: $^1/_2$, for example
✳ Used to express a proportion of something or a percentage

Some say I should be sad because I'm broken, because I'm just a *fraction* of the number I used to be. Well, I may be divided, but I can still conquer! Let me tell you why.

Written like this: $^2/_3$—my numerator tells you how many equal portions I contain (two), while my denominator tells you how many equal parts make up a whole (three). It's a neat little system that leaves Decimal floundering! You see, $^2/_3$ also means $2 \div 3$, but put that into a calculator and you get 0.6666666—ugh, that's messy! And check this out: you can compare two fractions by finding the lowest common denominator. Take $^5/_6$ and $^7/_9$. Both denominators go equally into 18 (6 x 3; 9 x 2). Multiplying the top number by the same figure in each case (5 x 3; 7 x 2) makes $^{15}/_{18}$ and $^{14}/_{18}$, so $^5/_6$ is "fraction"-ally the bigger portion.

● Proper fraction: numerator smaller than denominator ($^3/_5$)
● Improper fraction: numerator larger than denominator ($^7/_5$)
● Mixed number: whole number plus proper fraction ($1\,^2/_5$)

Fraction

Decimal

Number Nuts

* Form of not-whole number that is expressed using a period
* Takes its name from the Latin for tenth: *decimus*
* Works hand-in-hand with base 10

Hi, I'm Decimal, your pocket calculator pal. Just punch in 0.7734 and turn that gizmo upside down to get a big hello from me! Welcome to my universe.

Like Fraction, I inhabit the huge worlds that exist between whole numbers, but I'm more methodical than that pile of bulky numbers. Instead of denominators of all sizes, I use powers of ten. This means that I can convert stack-'em-high fractions into lovely decimal-digit strings. I transform $^4/_5$ into a neat 0.8, which ('cause you're pretty darn smart) you'll see is the same as $^8/_{10}$ or 8 ÷ 10. With me, messy mixed numbers, such as $3^1/_{12}$, are a thing of the past (3.083), and percentages are a cinch. Just look at 0.75 and you can see right away that it is $^{75}/_{100}$, or 75%. Try 0.04*. That's me—a straight-talking guy who likes to get to the point!

● Earliest known use: 1 B.C. (China)
● $^1/_2$ = 0.5
● *0.04 as a percentage: 4%

34

Decimal

Rational Number

Number Nuts

* Any number that can also be written as a fraction
* Finishes neatly or ends with a repeating pattern of numbers
* Includes all base 10 and base 2 numbers

I'm a reasonable fellow—I just like to see a pattern emerging. Rational, in math, refers to the ratio of two whole numbers—one divided by the other. My great pals are Integer, who is always divisible by 1 ($^{13}/_1$ is just 13, isn't it?), and Fraction—simply one integer over another. Okay, so $^2/_9$ makes a long repeating pattern in Decimal's hands*, but it is a pattern nonetheless.

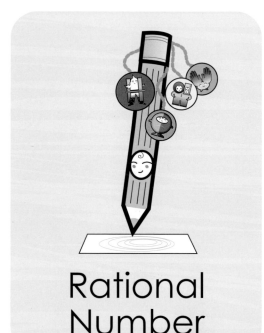

Rational Number

- $^{62}/_{99} = 0.6262626262$
- **Q:** the symbol used to denote the set of all rational numbers
- *2 ÷ 9 = 0.222222222222222

Irrational Number

Number Nuts

* Any number that cannot be written as a fraction
* Has an infinitely long decimal tail that never repeats
* Significantly more numbers are irrational than rational

Irrational
Number

I'm a nonstop nut that simply *can't* be written down as one whole number divided by another. Divide 4 by 1 and you get 0.25—a nice, well-rounded, rational decimal. But there's no end to my trailing decimal digits and no repeating patterns, either—count backward and you'll still be going at the end of time. My best buddies are Square Root, Pi, and e. You should check 'em out.

* $\sqrt{2}$: 1.414213562373095 . . .
* Pi (π): 3.141592653589793 . . .
* e: 2.718281828459045 . . .

Imaginary Number

Number Nuts

✳ One of math's most baffling concepts
✳ Used with real numbers to form complex numbers
✳ Labeled i to mean the square root of -1 ($\sqrt{-1}$)

Man the mizzenmasts and set sail for the strange lands of mathematical mystery! I'm a buccaneer of the bizarre—a totally unreal adventurer. My numbers don't belong to the real world of cookies and candy, but they are concrete and countable, nevertheless . . . stick with it!

You can tell if a number is imaginary because it has an i after it ($2i$), where the i is defined as $\sqrt{-1}$. And $\sqrt{-1}$ must be imaginary, mustn't it, because the square of any number is always positive, isn't it? Well, test it out: $-1 \times -1 = +1$. Mmm, yet my feet are firmly in the real world. Complex numbers, with their real and imaginary dimensions ($5 + 2i$), are perfect for describing electromagnetic radiation, such as sunlight or radio waves. I explode so many knotty real-world problems, I'm a weapon of *math* destruction!

● $i^2 = -1$ ($i \times i$, or i squared $= -1$)
● Inventor of i symbol: Leonhard Euler (1777)
● Euler's Theory: $e^{\pi i} = -1$ (e to the power of pi and $i = -1$)

Imaginary Number

CHAPTER 3
Cranium Crackers

This gang of brainy busters is awesome. The Cranium Crackers challenge you to use the stuffing between your ears—there's no room for scarecrow brains here! An incredible mix of extraordinary equations, fabulous functions, and punchy processes, these guys have amazing power to change numbers, push them about, split them up, and juggle them around. You will use each of them again and again when you do algebra, so find out how and why each of them operates (and how to reverse it). Before you know it, you'll be chipping away at tricky conundrums as if you were adding 1 + 1!

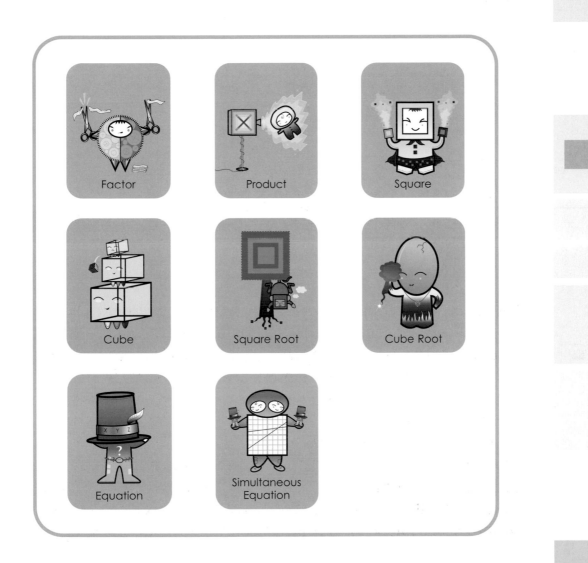

Factor

Product

Square

Cube

Square Root

Cube Root

Equation

Simultaneous
Equation

Factor

■ Cranium Crackers

☀ A positive integer that divides a larger number evenly
☀ Has no messy leftovers or remainders
☀ A number with factors of just 1 and itself is a prime number

AKA The Divisor, I'm a mean, green calculatin' machine. I blast a number into smaller, equal-size portions. Because there are often more than two ways to divide a number like this, the bigger the number, the more of me there are. For example, the number 9 has three factors (1, 3, and 9), while 32 has six factors (1, 2, 4, 8, 16, and 32).

Figuring out factors of really big numbers is as easy as nailing Jell-O to the wall. It takes some serious number crunching. The best way to do it is to split a number into its prime factors. Taking 737 and starting with the smallest prime numbers, you find that 737 will not divide by 2, 3, 5, or 7, but 11 x 67 = 737. It doesn't divide evenly by any other prime. So, 737 is a composite number with just four factors—1, 11, 67, and 737. Consider it crunched!

● If a number ends in 5 or 0, one of its factors is certainly 5
● Composite: the name given to a number with more than two factors
● Prime factor: any factor that is also a prime number

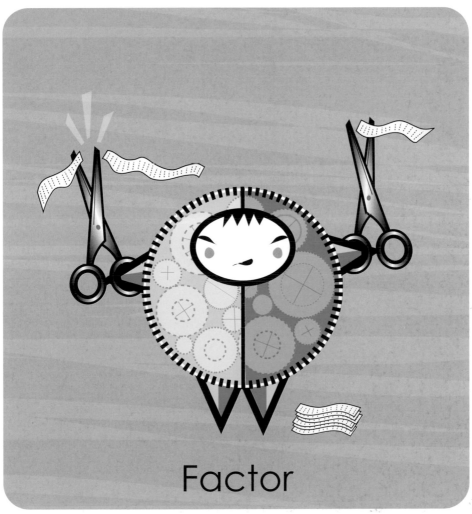

Factor

Product
■ Cranium Crackers

✳ The mathematical opposite of factor
✳ Also referred to as the result of one number times another
✳ Almost always a composite number and sometimes a prime

Hi, I'm Product—the apple to Factor's mathematical orange, and the Tom to his arithmetical Jerry. Whereas Factor is all about dividing numbers down to their smallest parts, I'm what you get when you multiply numbers together. Take 5 x 6 and you get a *product* of 30.

My job is all about thinking BIG (unless Negative Number happens to be involved)! And I'm hardly giving away any secrets when I say that numbers multiplied together to make a product are also the factors of that same product. I produce composite numbers—that is, any positive whole numbers with more factors than 1 and the number itself. Making prime numbers is trickier, because the only way to do it is by using 1 as a factor. Take 13. I can only make 13 as a product by multiplying 13 by 1 (13 x 1 = 13).

● Factorial (*n*!): product of the integers equal to and less than *n*
● 2 factorial (2!): 2 (2 x 1)
● 5 factorial (5!): 120 (5 x 4 x 3 x 2 x 1)

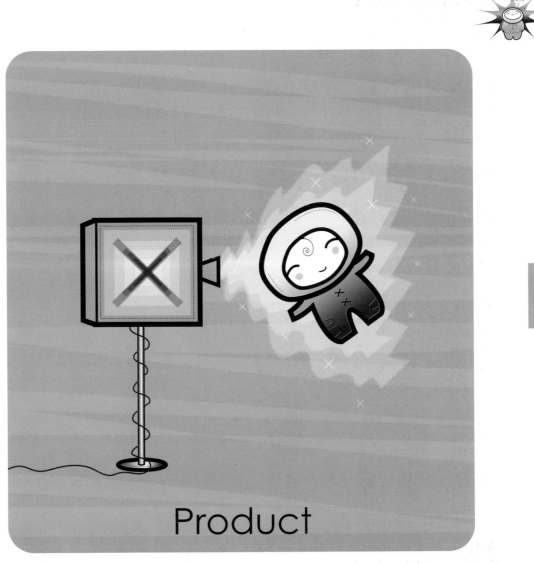

Product

Square

■ Cranium Crackers

※ A number multiplied by itself
※ A special case of power, where the index is two
※ The mathematical opposite of square root

Call me Square Pants if you want, but I'm far from boring. The littlest of the Power pals, I'm a number raised to the power of two (that is, multiplied by itself). Two squared is 2^2. It's the same as 2 x 2 = 4. I'm always positive*—but you know that by now. When I square Odd Number, the result is odd—while squares of Even Number are even. I have my uses, so you'd better *square* up.

Square

● Units squared are used to measure area—for example, $ft.^2$ or m^2
● All squares end in a repeating pattern: 00, 1, 4, 9, 6, 25, 6, 9, 4, 1, 00
● *3^2: (3 x 3) = 9 and -3^2: (-3 x -3) = 9

Cube

Cranium Crackers ■

✴ A number multiplied by itself and then again
✴ A special case of power, where the power index is three
✴ The mathematical opposite of cube root

Cube

Imagine a Rubik's Cube and you've got me—a solid shape where each side is equal to three units. Officially, I'm a number raised to the power of three. This just means a number multiplied by itself and then multiplied by itself again. Two cubed is 2^3, which is the same as $2 \times 2 \times 2 = 8$. There's more to me than my bro, Square, and, unlike him, I can be a little negative* at times.

● Units multiplied in three dimensions give you the volume of a solid shape
● Smallest cube that is a sum of two different cubes is 1,729: $1^3 + 12^3 = 9^3 + 10^3$
● *3^3: $(3 \times 3 \times 3) = 27$, but -3^3: $(-3 \times -3 \times -3) = -27$

Square Root
■ Cranium Crackers

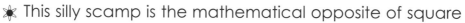

☀ This silly scamp is the mathematical opposite of square
☀ The square root of −1 ($\sqrt{-1}$) is an imaginary number (*i*)
☀ A natural number has a positive and a negative square root

A mathematical monkey, I swing my tail over a number to undo Square's multiplication: $4^2 = 16$ and $\sqrt{16} = 4$. The definition for $\sqrt{x}$ is the number whose square equals x: so $\sqrt{16} = 4$. When given a perfect square like 16, I'll make a lovely rational number (4). But try me on nonperfect squares—say, 15*—and I'll give you endless (literally) irrational numbers.

Square Root

● Earliest known use: between 1800 B.C. and 1600 B.C. (Babylon)
● $\sqrt{x} = x^{1/2}$
● *$\sqrt{15} = 3.872983346207416 \ldots$

Cube Root
Cranium Crackers

* This egghead is the mathematical opposite of cube
* Cube roots of nonperfect cubes are irrational numbers
* Any (real) number has only one cube root

Cube Root

Like Square Root, I'm a real hotshot, busy undoing all of Cube's hard work. See how quickly I unpick Cube's multiplication: $4^3 = 64$ and $\sqrt[3]{64} = 4$. Ha ha. Nothing could be easier, could it? The definition for $\sqrt[3]{x}$ is the number whose cube equals x: so $\sqrt[3]{64} = 4$. Unlike Square, I can only ever have one root— I'll have none of this positive/negative roots business. No sir!

● First demonstrated by Galileo (1638)
● $\sqrt[3]{x} = x^{1/3}$
● On a calculator: press √, x, √√, x, √√√, x, etc. until the number doesn't change

Equation

■ Cranium Crackers

✳ Algebraic method where letters replace unknown numbers
✳ Defines a relationship between one or more variables
✳ Expressions on either side of the equal sign have the same value

I've got a bad rep for being a complicated brain acher. But given the chance, I can show you how to use letters instead of numbers to think in a new and exciting way.

Sometimes, you have an answer but don't know the question. At these times, my letters stand in for the numbers that you don't know. Say Tyson is 4 years old and Rosie is 26. At what age will Rosie be three times Tyson's age? Well, in x years from now, Tyson will be $4 + x$ and Rosie will be $26 + x$. Written as an equation, she will be three times older than he is when $3(4 + x) = 26 + x$. You can eliminate the numbers that you *do* know by writing the same equation like this: $26 - (3 \times 4) = 2x$. So now you know that $14 = 2x$, which means that $x = 7$. When Tyson is 11, Rosie will be 33. It's as easy as *a, b, c*—or should I say *x, y, z*!

● A linear equation has only one value of x that will solve it
● A quadratic equation is one that involves a square
● A cubic equation is one that involves a cube

Equation

51

Simultaneous Equation

■ Cranium Crackers

✳ Finds solutions for two (or more) separate equations
✳ Works by substituting one equation into another
✳ Can also be solved by plotting it on a graph

I am algebra's elder statesman, a multitasker whose left hand *always* knows what the right hand is doing. I help out when two (or more) equations need a mutual solution.

When faced with two equations, say $3x + 2y = 8$ and $x + 4y = 6$, you must first know that solutions exist that make them *both* true. The key is to isolate one of the variables. In this case, $3x + 2y = 8$ looks tricky, but $x + 4y = 6$ can be rewritten as $x = 6 - 4y$ (isolating the x). The first equation can now read as $3(6 - 4y) + 2y = 8$. Distributing the 3 on the parentheses gives you $18 - 12y + 2y = 8$. Simplified further, this is $18 - 10y = 8$, which can also be written $10y = 18 - 8$. This means that $10y = 10$, so $y = 1$. Now *you* return to the second equation to find x*!

● First known use: c. 1950 B.C. (Babylon)
● Father of algebra: Muhammad ibn Musa al-Khwarizmi (c. A.D. 780–850)
● *$x + 4y = 6$: $x + (4 \times 1) = 6$, so $x + 4 = 6$ or $x = 6 - 4$; $x = 2$

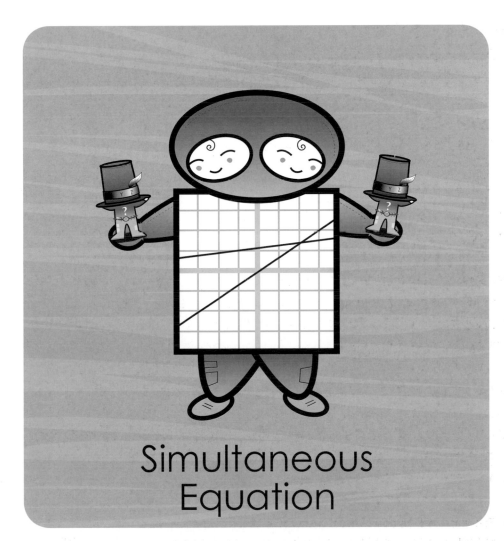

Simultaneous
Equation

CHAPTER 4
Graph Gang

Bring out the Graph Gang! This hands-on bunch of mathematical wonders simply love to roll up their sleeves, sharpen their pencils, and get something down on graph paper. These guys prove the point that by far the best way to visualize a math formula is to do it graphically. It's a team effort, with stalwarts Line, Plane, and Function *coordinating* (get it?) their energies to show the relationship between two (or more) variables in an equation (that is, how y varies with x). Literally *drawing* together their incredible powers makes them amazing at analyzing data. Seeing really *is* believing!

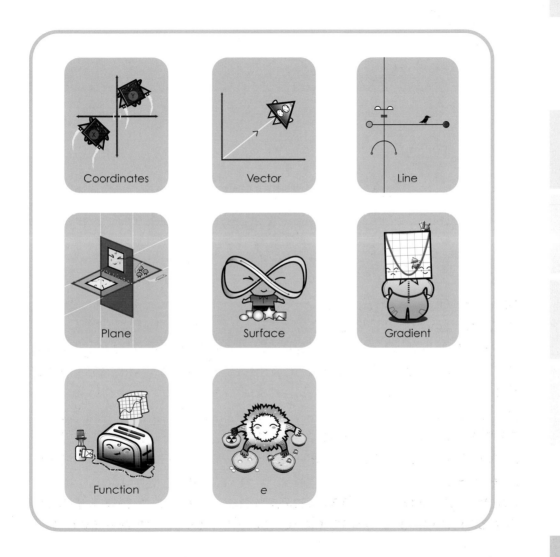

Coordinates

Vector

Line

Plane

Surface

Gradient

Function

e

Coordinates

■ Graph Gang

* Pairs of numbers, written (x,y), locating position
* The x-axis is horizontal, and the y-axis is vertical
* They provide grid references so that mapmaking is possible

Location, location, location—it's what we're all about. You see, we provide a system for pinpointing a position. It's great—you'll never be lost with us around!

We're called x and y, and although we're small, the Graph Gang would get nowhere without us. Every single one of them needs *us* to be able to conduct their operations. This is how we work: x is positioned on the horizontal axis, while y is positioned on the vertical axis. The point at which our lines cross gives a position, which is written down as two numbers inside parentheses, separated by a comma: (4,3) or (–5,7). Our values are written in alphabetical order, so the first number refers to the x coordinate and the second number to the y coordinate. Oh yeah, we have it all mapped out!

● Inventor: René Descartes (1600s)
● Formal name: Cartesian coordinates (from Descartes)
● The coordinates (0,0) are labeled as "the origin"

Coordinates

Vector
■ Graph Gang

✳ A line on a graph that has magnitude (size) and direction
✳ Works with coordinates to get from point to point on a graph
✳ Vectors with the same magnitude and direction are equal

I'm a zippy little fellow that's drawn as a straight line on a graph. I get you from point to point using the shortest distance and, believe me, I know where I'm going!

I'm a double decker, written with one number stacked on top of the other in parentheses. I use my pals, Coordinates, with my x value above my y value. So $\binom{3}{4}$ means move three across to the right (in a positive x direction) and move four up the y-axis. When you see me on a graph, there's a chevron, or arrow, drawn on my line to indicate direction. The very same line in the opposite direction is $\binom{-3}{-4}$ and has a downward-pointing arrow. I can be added, subtracted, *and* multiplied—engineers adore me! They use me to calculate the results of forces acting in different directions. Don't hector this Vector!

● Vector graphics: computer images drawn using geometry rather than pixels
● First video game: Spacewar! (Steve "Slug" Russell, 1961)
● First vector graphics drawing program: Sketchpad (1963)

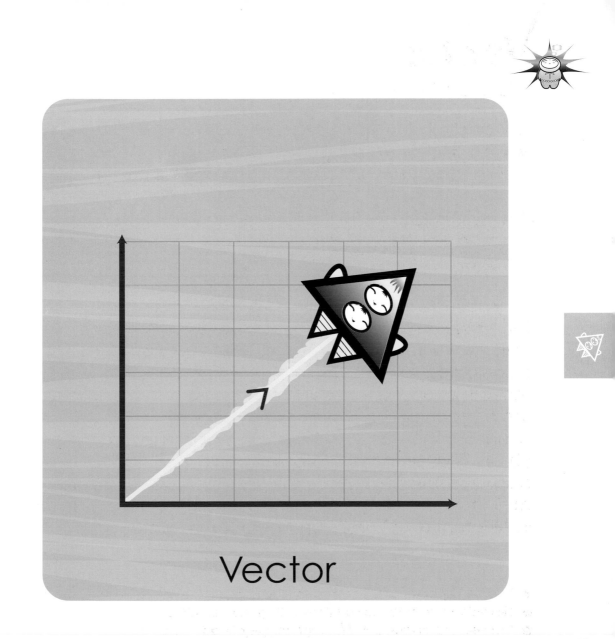

Vector

Line
■ Graph Gang

- ✳ A one-dimensional character of infinite length
- ✳ Linear functions (equations) draw clean, straight lines
- ✳ Quadratic and cubic functions draw beautiful curves

I'm a stringbean of a guy—the skinniest beanpole you ever did see. I'm so thin, I exist in one dimension only! I have no width or depth, only length. But no matter how flimsy and wobbly you think I am, there's not a shape or function that can be drawn without me.

I can be straight or curved. When I'm straight, I take the shortest route between two points (like Vector), while my curved versions arc elegantly across the page. I am drawn toward other lines (unless they are parallel, two straight lines always meet). And when I intersect, or cross, another line, I make an angle—for example, perpendicular lines meet at right angles (90°). Meanwhile, parallel lines run like train tracks—on and on, side by side, never getting closer to each other and never getting farther away. Ahh!

- ● Line segment: a line of fixed length with two end points
- ● Hyperbola and parabola: names given to special curved lines
- ● Spirangle: a spiral made using straight lines

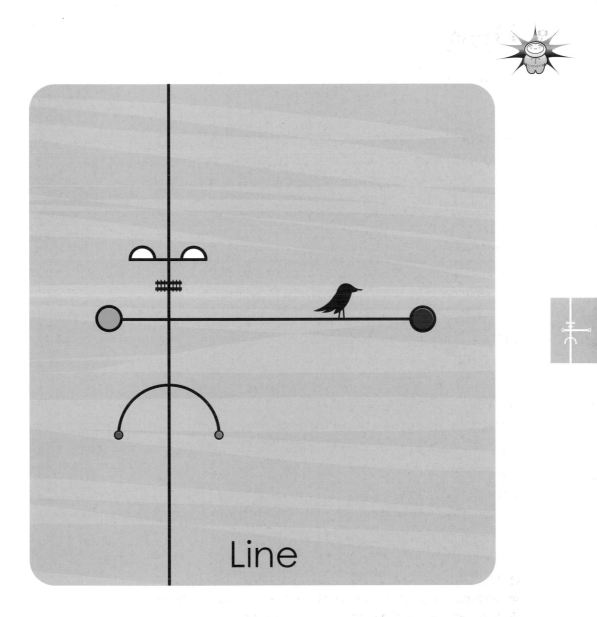

Line

Plane
■ Graph Gang

✳ A 2-D surface of infinite area and zero thickness
✳ Two nonparallel planes will always intersect along a line
✳ A line can intersect a plane, run parallel to it, or be part of it

Imagine a wall, floor, or ceiling stretching out forever in every direction to make me: beautiful Plane. Mmm, no doubt you are looking at that wall, floor, or ceiling, all flat and featureless, and wondering what's so special. But, really, there's more to me than meets the eye.

You see, a graph—most geometry, in fact—is carried out in the plane: lines are drawn across my surface. Like Line, I can be parallel, where one plane sits above another, like stacked sheets of paper. They never get closer to each other or move farther away, and they most certainly do not touch! I also intersect with other planes to make solid shapes with flat surfaces. Perpendicular planes intersect at right angles to make cuboid shapes, but I can also make prisms and pyramids. You see, I'm no *plane* Jane after all!

● World's largest ice rink: 1,782,504 ft.² (165,600m²) (Rideau Canal Skateway, Canada)
● World's largest flat-screen TV: 15.7 x 7.9 ft. (4.8 x 2.4m) (Technovision Luxio)
● World's longest covered outdoor escalator system: 2,625 ft. (800m) (Hong Kong)

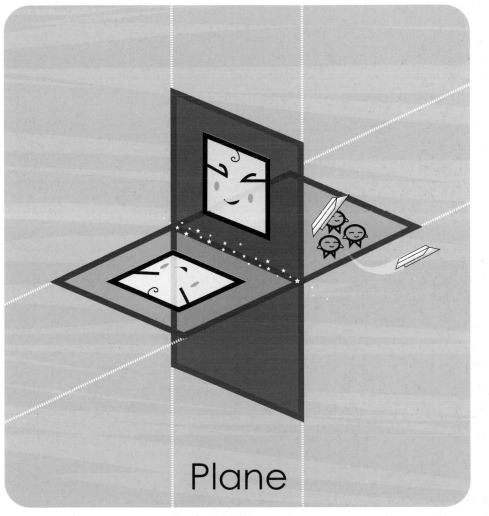

Plane

Surface
■ Graph Gang

✴ A 2-D area of zero thickness, sometimes curved in 3-D space
✴ Stretches like a skin over every 3-D shape
✴ Surfaces with edges and a fixed area are said to be "closed"

Check me out! I'm the ultimate in geometry flamboyancy. Math geeks go gaga for my curves! Unlike simpletons Line and Plane, I can also work in three dimensions.

I make up the outer walls of a solid shape: every single object has me stretched over its outsides. While you can visualize Plane with something as disappointing as a wall, you can picture my sweeping curves on a rounded shape like a cylinder. Wanna see a trick? Take a long strip of paper, twist it in the middle, and connect the ends together to make a loop. Run your finger all the way around that loop and you'll see that you've made a special shape with only one surface. While fun, this frivolity merely scratches at the *surface* of the computing and engineering applications I can help with.

● First described: c. 300 B.C. (Euclid)
● Surface area of a cube: $6s^2$ (s is length of one side)
● Total surface area of an average adult brain: 388 in.^{2} (2,500cm^2)

Surface

Gradient

■ Graph Gang

✳ The slope of a line on a graph
✳ A positive gradient slopes up from left to right
✳ A negative gradient slides down from left to right

Hey, come climb with me, the concept with very real effects. The bigger the gradient of a hill, the steeper it is and the more you'll sweat as you go! There's no goofing off here—this ride is for mountain goats only!

I'm a cinch to calculate. The gradient of a slope—real or mathematical, steep or shallow—is the ratio between how far you climb up (the vertical, y component) and the distance you travel forward (the horizontal, x component). In math language, this is written $(y_2-y_1)/(x_2-x_1)$. To find the gradient of a straight line, therefore, all you do is find two points on it and figure out the difference between their y and x components. Say the two points were (3,2) and (8,4). I would be $4^{-2}/8^{-3} = {}^2/_5 = 0.4$ (also written as two in five, 2:5, or 40%). Well, get moving! Can you make the grade?

● Gradient of 1 is equal to a 45° angle on a standard coordinate grid
● Steepest (nonrack) train track: 0.135 (13.5%), Lisbon, Portugal
● Steepest rack railroad: 0.48 (48%), Pilatus Mountain Railway, Switzerland

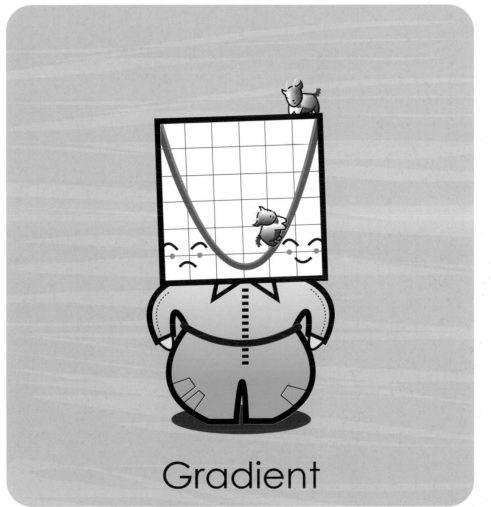

Gradient

Function

■ Graph Gang

✳ A formula that converts one value into another
✳ An inverse function reverses the operation
✳ All functions are equations, but not all equations are functions

I'm an operator, a hustler, and a mathematical string puller. I work the numbers, taking one value and changing it into another. I am written as $f(x)$, which is spoken as "eff of ex." Whenever you see me, you know you are looking at an equation of some kind, written in terms of x. Put simply, plug x into the equation and out pops an answer.

There's nothing to be scared of here. My operations can be as simple as adding 1 to a number. Take $f(x) = 3x + 1$: if x is 7, $f(x) = 22$ (that is, $3 \times 7 + 1$). Easy, right? Loads of guys in this book can be described as forms of me: Square, Cube, Sine, Cosine, Tangent, Square Root, Cube Root—they're all functions! Square is just an easier way of saying $f(x) = x$ times x. I come into my own on a graph, helping draw all kinds of lines, curves, and shapes.

● First use of the word *function*: 1673 (Gottfried Leibniz)
● Linear functions (x) produce straight-line graphs
● Quadratic functions (x^2) produce parabolic (curved-line) graphs

Function

e

■ Graph Gang

✳ The most important and useful constant in math
✳ Defined as the limit of $(1 + 1/n)^n$ as n goes to infinity
✳ Crops up anywhere there is growth or decay

A relative newcomer to math, I am sparky and vibrant. My full name is Euler's Number (after that brainy fellow Leonhard Euler, who investigated my many and various uses). You can call me e. I am the most important number, along with 0 (Zero), 1 (Unity), π (Pi), and i (Imaginary Number). Like my good friend Pi, I am a mathematical constant and an Irrational Number to boot!

I'm used for measuring things that grow continuously, and I put a limit on how fast they flourish. And, believe me, I have a finger in a lot of pies. Give me half a chance and I'll tell you how radioactive decay slows down or the maximum your money can earn in a bank. I can even be used to find out how quickly a deadly virus could spread. All together now—"For e's a jolly good fellow!"

● Discoverer: Jacob Bernoulli (1727)
● Euler's Number (e): 2.71828182845904523536 . . .
● Known digits of e: 1,000,000,000,000 decimal places (Kondo & Yee, 2010)

e

CHAPTER 5
Shape Sisters

What a bunch of beauties the Shape Sisters are, with the lovely Polygon leading by example. Lying flat on a 2-D plane, Polygon is made with straight lines that meet at points, or vertices. The smallest shape that can be made in this way is a triangle (spot the family connection with the Trig-Athletes). Besides shapely shapes, this sisterhood embraces 1-D Perimeter, 2-D and 3-D spaceheads Area and Volume, and playful, pattern-making Tessellation. Together, they let you explore the world of shapes—for example, out of all four-sided shapes with the same Perimeter, a square has the largest Area. Square that!

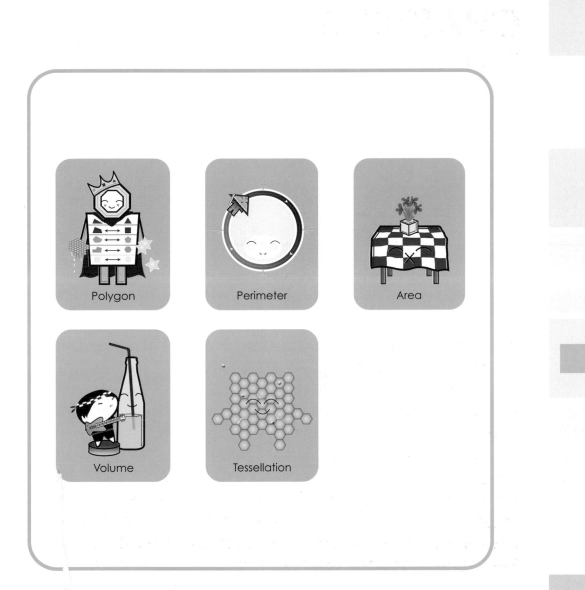

Polygon

Perimeter

Area

Volume

Tessellation

Polygon
■ Shape Sisters

✴ A shape made using points, straight lines, and angles
✴ Each point, or corner, on a polygon is called a vertex
✴ From the Greek *polygon*, meaning figure with many angles

All hail the queen of the 2-D flatlands! I am known as the set of all shapes, which means that every shape you can think of that is made with straight lines is one of me. You could say I'm the *shape* of things to come. Ha ha!

I can be regular or irregular, and it doesn't take long to spot the difference. Irregular, and I'm a jumble with sides of different lengths and crazy interior angles. Regular, though, and there's a little more finesse: my sides are all exactly the same length and all interior angles are equal. You'll see regular polygons everywhere—in starfruit (pentagon) and honeycombs (hexagon), for example. When laid next to each other, some shapes of the same kind fit together snugly with no gaps. It's a great game that Tessellation will tell you all about later or .

● *n*-gon: a polygon with *n* sides (*pentagon*, 5; *hexagon*, 6)
● All interior angles of a quadrilateral must add up to 360°
● Polyhedron (*pl.* polyhedra): a solid whose faces are polygons

Polygon

Perimeter
■ Shape Sisters

☀ The distance around the outside of an area
☀ Without this boundary, there is no shape
☀ The perimeter of a circle is known as its circumference

Come on out, I have you surrounded! No, seriously, just giving you the runaround. It's what I do—I draw a line that encloses a shape to form its outline. I give a shape definition. That's me, a real mover and shaper!

I'm just the thing you need for figuring out the area of chicken wire required for your rabbit hutch or the length of sparkly fabric to run around the hem of your skirt. Yes, but how? Well, take any shape, flatten out its edges, and measure their length. For quadrilaterals (four-sided shapes like squares and rectangles), it's pretty easy to add up all four sides. Geometry tells us that if opposite interior angles are the same, opposite sides are equal in length. For triangles, you'll need help from the Pythagorean Theorem, Sine, Cosine, and Tangent . . . maybe later!

● Perimeter of a regular polygon: $2nb\sin^{\pi}/_n$
● n = number of sides; b = distance from the center to one of the vertices
● Largest country perimeter (coastline): 125,567 mi. (202,080km) (Canada)

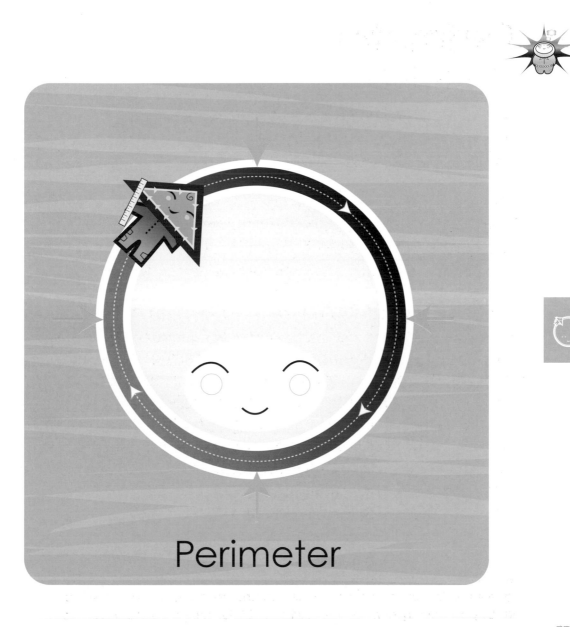

Perimeter

Area

■ Shape Sisters

✳ Provides the measure of a 2-D space
✳ Can be applied to flat shapes and 3-D surfaces
✳ Always measured in square units—e.g. in.², ft.², cm², m²

I love to get the measure of things. Just give me the chance and I'll tell you the exact size of *any* flat shape you want, using *any* square unit you like. Hey, I may be square by name, but I'm not square by nature!

You already know that Line has one dimension (length). Well, I can tell you that a flat shape has two dimensions (length plus width or height). I measure the space within these dimensions—Area—by multiplying one by the other. I can tell you the size of your favorite cookie or how big a poster you need to hide that splat mark. I can also give you the area of a 3-D object—Surface—by curving around a cylinder or spreading like a cloth over a set table, accounting for every lump and bump over the plates, silverware, and candles. Oh yeah, I've got it *covered*!

● Area of a square or rectangle: A = base x height
● Area of a triangle: A = base x height ÷ 2
● Area of the world's largest country: 6,601,668 mi.² (17,098,242 km²) (Russia)

Area

Volume
■ Shape Sisters

✳ Measures the amount of space taken up by a 3-D shape
✳ Used for measuring the capacity of containers
✳ Measured in cubic units (ft.³, mi.³) or gallons, liters, etc.

There are no two ways about it, I've sure got bulk. My 3-D outlines epitomize my voluptuous nature. Nobody's as good at taking up space as I am!

Let's get one thing straight: being loud is not my thing. My interest lies in how much space a 3-D shape takes up or the amount of liquid or gas it would hold if it were hollow and filled right to the brim—I'm talking capacity. I multiply a shape's three dimensions—length, height, and depth— to find out. Incidentally, did you know that there are only five perfectly regular 3-D shapes with equal sides, angles, and matching faces? Yep—tetrahedron (4 triangles), cube (6 squares), octahedron (8 triangles), dodecahedron (12 pentagons), and icosahedron (20 triangles). Wow! My *capacity* for knowledge simply astounds me!

● Volume of a pyramid: V = $^{Bh}/_3$ (B = area of base; h = height of pyramid)
● Volume of a prism: V = Al (area of cross section x length)
● Volume and capacity (in metric system): 1,000cm³ = 1 liter; 1cm³ = 1 milliliter

Volume

Tessellation
■ Shape Sisters

✳ This puzzler fits shapes together edge to edge
✳ If a shape tessellates, the angles around a point make 360°
✳ In Latin, *tessella* means a small, cubical piece of mosaic tiling

I'm a real puzzler. I just love playing around with shapes to see what patterns I can make. I fit them together so that there are no gaps or overlaps between their edges.

I've been around for centuries, making intricate patterns for Islamic tile decorations, Roman mosaics, and M. C. Escher's astounding mathematical graphic art, among other things. I can make regular patterns in a flash, using equilateral triangles, squares, or hexagons. In a more flamboyant mood, I work with two or more shapes—squares, triangles, or other polygons—to make semiregular patterns. There's a knack to making nonidentical vertices add up to 360° around a given point, I can tell you! For a real workout, I make 3-D puzzles where different-shaped blocks slot together to make a solid cube. How fitting!

● Regular tessellation: shapes must fill space with no overlaps and no gaps
● Regular tessellation: shapes must all be identical regular polygons
● Regular tessellation: all vertices must look the same

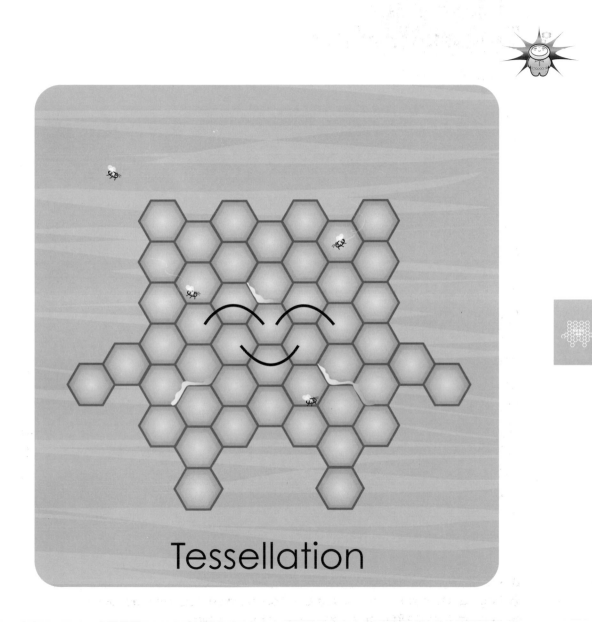

Tessellation

CHAPTER 6
Transformation Team

Boom! Time to meet the sumo-size movers and shakers of the math world. The Transformation Team is a rough-and-tumble wrestling outfit whose members excel when it comes to making a *move*. These guys are shape-shifters, literally changing the way a shape looks. Each larger-than-life character has a super skill, from Translation's shove tactics and Rotation's spinning maneuvers to Reflection's mirror images and Enlargement's resizing tricks. The Graph Gang keep all of these tumbling transformations in check. Keep in step with this group and they'll really get you into shape!

Translation

Rotation

Reflection

Enlargement

Symmetry

Translation
■ Transformation Team

✴ Moves geometrical shapes without warping them
✴ Works with vector to produce sliding movements
✴ Size, shape, or orientation of a shape remains unchanged

Ohayo! I am the sumo Numero Uno of this outfit, and my special move is the shove. I have the power to push a shape around. I don't mess with its size or rearrange its looks, I just slide it from one place to another. Being in the ring with me is a very *moving* experience!

My simplest transformation is to move a single point from *here* to *there*. It's a movement that has both distance and direction. Ring any bells? Yep, good old Vector helps out. Say I want to move a point with coordinates (0,3) up four and along three. Well, Vector just adds $\binom{4}{3}$ to (0,3) to get the new coordinates (4,6). Once you've mastered that little trick, you'll be pushing shapes all over the place. Just remember to give each point a shove by the same distance and in the same direction.

● **T:** the symbol used to denote the set of all translations
● Positive coordinates move a point up or to the right
● Negative coordinates move a point down or to the left

Translation

Rotation
■ Transformation Team

※ Spins a shape around a fixed point—the center of rotation
※ Changes the direction in which some shapes point
※ Shape remains the same size and shape

Meet Sumo #2. *Konnichiwa!* While Translation shoves a shape from A to B, I prefer to send it in a spin. I pick it up and twirl it around like it's a drum majorette's baton.

I don't change the size or outline of a shape, but I do alter its orientation—that is, which way up it is or whether it faces left or right. So, when I pivot a triangle, all of its corners could end up in different positions. It could look different from the way it did before rotation, although it is still exactly the same shape and size. Anything that spins—a bike wheel, say—rotates around a fixed point, and that's how I operate. First, I find the point around which the shape should be rotated. If the center of rotation lies *inside* the shape, it will spin like a wheel; if it lies *outside*, it will act more like a bucket on a rope. Face it, I'm great all *around*.

● Quarter turn (right angle): 90°
● Half turn (straight line): 180°
● Full turn (circle): 360°

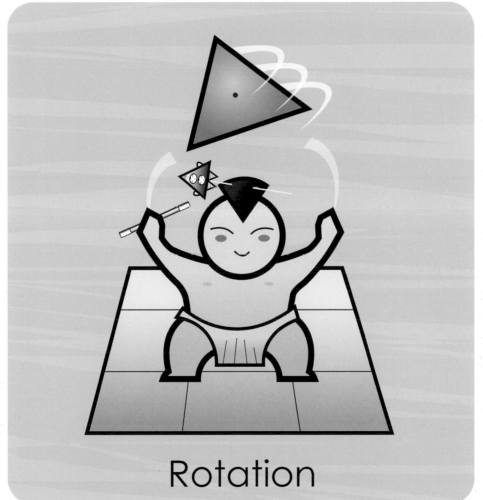

Rotation

Reflection

■ Transformation Team

★ Holds a mirror up to shapes and shows their reflections
★ Cannot be achieved simply by sliding or turning
★ A reflection is always the same distance from the mirror's axis

I'm *flipping* crazy! I'm Sumo #3 and I'm more loony than the two heavyweights you've met so far. *Konbanwa!* When it comes to shapes, I'm not content just to shove or spin 'em around. No, I flip 'em right over like pancakes!

I am what happens when you look in the mirror—go on, give it a try. It looks as if your left and right sides have switched over, but this can't be the case, can it? In fact, what has happened is that the image facing you is back to front. Ouch! Instead of a mirror, I use a line on a graph— say the x-axis or the y-axis. Try to imagine that my line is the central crease of an open book. Think of the mark a shape would leave on the opposite page if you closed the book while the ink was still wet and you've got me! Time to pause for a little *reflection*, I think!

● Reflection symmetry: describes a shape reflected along an axis
● $x = c$ describes a reflection on the vertical axis
● $y = c$ describes a reflection on the horizontal axis

Reflection

Enlargement
■ Transformation Team

✳ Increases (or decreases) the size of a shape
✳ Action takes place around a center of enlargement
✳ Uses scale factor to show size of enlargement (or shrinkage)

Watch out, Sumo #4 is here. *Hajimemashite!* Among this team's sumo superstars, I have the greatest effect on shapes—I blow them up! *Pow!* I slash their area. *Slam!*

My shape-busting moves employ a slick combination of scale factor plus center of enlargement (COE). Scale factor determines how many times bigger (or smaller) the transformed shape is, while the COE is the point from which the enlargement is made. A line drawn through each corner of the original shape and its corresponding corner on the enlargement will converge at the COE. Uniform scaling (equal enlargement in all directions) creates an identical shape, while nonuniform scaling (using more than one scale factor) can stretch or squeeze a shape's proportions. That's me, I like to *stretch a point*!

● Scale factor of 1: no enlargement or reduction (same shape)
● Scale factor greater than 1: an increase in size (positive enlargement)
● Scale factor between −1 and 1: a decrease in size (negative enlargement)

Enlargement

Symmetry
Transformation Team

* When a shape remains unchanged by rotation or translation
* AKA reflection symmetry, line symmetry, or mirror symmetry
* All regular polygons have a least one line of symmetry

Unlike the heavies of the Transformation Team, I'm more of a thinker than a doer. I study the properties of each shape I encounter, looking for a certain kind of similarity.

I draw a line down or across a shape in such a way that it has exactly similar parts facing each other. A line drawn down the center of a square, for example, makes two identical upright rectangles side by side. Draw a line across the center of that square and you get identical rectangles on top of one another. A line from corner to corner makes two exact same triangles, and so on. This little trick is called reflection symmetry, but I can also *turn* my hand to rotational symmetry: spin a square around its center point and it looks exactly the same in four positions. It's perfect symmetry, I tell you, so *sayonara* from Sumo #5.

● Shape with the highest number of lines of symmetry: circle
● 1-D shapes have a *point* of symmetry, 2-D shapes an *axis*, and 3-D shapes a *plane*
● Opposite of symmetry/symmetrical: asymmetry/asymmetrical

Symmetry

95

CHAPTER 7
Trig-Athletes

Welcome to the ancient mathematical field they call trigonometry (from the Greek for triangle measurement). Like all things ancient Greek, the Trig-Athletes love shapes, philosophical arguments, and physical competitions. In their world, lines come together to make Angle and three different types of Triangle. Never far away, Sine, Cosine, and Tangent hang out with their old buddy Pythagorean Theorem. And what an obsessive bunch they are as they find Triangle's vital statistics—just how long are its sides? How big are those angles? And what's the area? Let's see how they're doing . . .

Angle

Triangle

Pythagorean
Theorem

Sine

Cosine

Tangent

Angle
Trig-Athletes

✳ Found at the point where two lines meet
✳ Marked by an arc and measured in degrees
✳ 360° is the angle in a complete turn—a full circle

Believe me, I'm no angel. Unless two lines are parallel, they always cross one another, and you'll find me where they meet. I loiter at the corners of geometrical shapes.

I've been around for centuries: as long as 4,000 years ago, the Sumerians and Babylonians used to love busting their brains with me. But that's ancient history; let's get to the *point*! I come in many flavors: acute, obtuse, right, straight, and reflex. When I'm acute, I'm tight, sharp, and less than 90°. Obtuse sees me playing wide and loose between 90° and 180°. When I'm right (and, boy, do I like to be right), I am halfway between being acute and obtuse, at 90° exactly. And when I'm straight, I sit on Line at precisely 180°. With reflex, I blow it wide open and flap away at angles from 180° to 360°.

● Angle of Earth's axis: about 23.5° from vertical
● Sum of exterior angles of all polygons: 360°
● Exterior angle of a regular polygon: $360 \div n$ (n = number of sides)

Angle

Triangle
Trig-Athletes

* A polygon with three vertices and three straight-line sides
* A favorite with engineers because of its strength
* Interior (inside) angles of triangles always add up to 180°

Rigid and strong, I'm not the sort of guy who takes kindly to being pushed around—just you *try* it. No, you'll find me reinforcing skyscrapers, bridges, and dams—places that require a certain kind of supporting structure.

Geometry buffs just love me and have devoted a whole field of study with a fancy name to my spiky shapes. It's called trigonometry. My most regular form is equilateral, with all sides the same length and a 60° angle in each corner. Scalene triangles are the exact opposite, with *no* equal angles or same-length sides. Isosceles triangles manage to have two sides the same and two equal angles, while right triangles famously have one 90°-angle corner. To figure out the lengths of my sides, you need to meet my fellow Trig-Athletes. Step this way . . .

● Area of a triangle: $A = \frac{1}{2}ab\sin(C)$ (*a*, *b* are any two sides, C is their angle)
● Vertices of the Bermuda Triangle: Bermuda, Florida, and Puerto Rico
● First triangular sandwich: 1765 (John Montagu, 4th Earl of Sandwich)

Triangle

Pythagorean Theorem
Trig-Athletes

* ☀ The world's most proven math formula
* ☀ Calculates the length of the sides of a right triangle
* ☀ The theorem says $a^2 + b^2 = c^2$

I am an amazing piece of mathematical magic credited to one of the greatest mathe*magicians* that ever lived— the ancient Greek genius Pythagoras (569–475 B.C.).

My mantra goes like this: "The sum of the squares of the legs of a right triangle is equal to the square of the hypotenuse." Rolls off the tongue, doesn't it! Okay, so let's get all things triangular sorted out: the hypotenuse is the longest side of a triangle and is always across from the 90° angle in a right triangle; the legs are the two sides that make that angle. If you know the length of the legs (*a* and *b*), you can find the length of the hypotenuse (*c*), using my formula $a^2 + b^2 = c^2$. That's more like it!

* ● Number of Pythagorean proofs known to exist: 145 (*Guinness Book of Records*)
* ● Famous Pythagorean provers: Prince Charles; U.S. President James A. Garfield
* ● Famous Pythagorean triples: {$a = 3$, $b = 4$, $c = 5$}; {$a = 5$, $b = 12$, $c = 13$}

Pythagorean
Theorem

Sine

Trig-Athletes

- The first of three trigonometric or circular functions
- Helps find side lengths and angles in right triangles
- Remembered as SOH (Sine = Opposite/Hypotenuse)

Wave bye-bye to the shallows, my friend. Strap me and my two brothers, Cosine and Tangent, to your side and head out into the mathematical deep waters.

I can show you how to get the measure of a right triangle when Pythagorean Theorem just isn't enough. Start by labeling the angles of the triangle A, B, and C. The longest side, the hypotenuse (hyp), is always opposite the right angle (C). The side opposite angle A is called the opposite (opp), and the side adjacent to angle A is called the adjacent (adj). Well, I am the ratio of the opposite divided by the hypotenuse. Using the formula sin A = $^{opp}/_{hyp}$, you can find out the lengths of the opposite and the hypotenuse sides when you know angle A and find out angle A when you know the sides. It's as simple as that!

- Law of sines: $\{^{a}/_{\sin A}\} = \{^{b}/_{\sin B}\} = \{^{c}/_{\sin C}\}$
- Mathematical abbreviation for sine: sin
- Drawn on a graph, the sine function makes a repeating wave pattern

hyp

opp

adj

Sine

Cosine
Trig-Athletes

- ✴ The second of three trigonometric or circular functions
- ✴ Helps find side lengths and angles in a triangle
- ✴ Remembered as CAH (Cosine = Adjacent/Hypotenuse)

I ain't no costar, baby. Sine might come first, but I'm never far behind. I'm known as the ratio of the adjacent side of a right triangle—the side nearest angle A—divided by the hypotenuse ($^{adj}/_{hyp}$). I combine explosively with Pythagorean Theorem to make the law of cosines, a mathematical super-weapon that holds true for any triangle, not just ones with right angles.

Cosine

- ● Law of cosines: $a^2 + b^2 - 2ab\cos C = c^2$
- ● Mathematical abbreviation for cosine: cos
- ● Like sine, cosine makes a repeating wave pattern when drawn on a graph

Tangent
Trig-Athletes

- ✳ The third of three trigonometric or circular functions
- ✳ Helps find side lengths and angles in a triangle
- ✳ Remembered as TOA (Tangent = Opposite/Adjacent)

Tangent

Always direct and to the point, I'm the odd one out of the trig triplets. I am defined as the ratio of the opposite divided by the adjacent ($^{opp}/_{adj}$). But because sin A=$^{opp}/_{hyp}$ and cos A=$^{adj}/_{hyp}$, I can also be written as $^{sin\ A}/_{cos\ A}$. Flexible, that's me. The graph of my function doesn't drone on in endless, mind-numbing waves—it makes short flicks from negative infinity into positive infinity.

- ● Law of Tangents: $\tan(A + B) = [\tan(A) + \tan(B)] \div [1 - (\tan A)(\tan B)]$
- ● Mathematical abbreviation for tangent: tan
- ● First use of abbreviations: 1626 (Albert Girard)

CHAPTER 8
In the Round

Time to meet the most pleasing group of 2-D and 3-D shapes. Pleasing, because they are based around the perfect circle. As well as Circle himself, gallant old Circumference will give you the right royal runaround. Then there's pretty Ellipse, chunky, barrel-chested Cylinder, cocky Cone, and serene Sphere! Woven into the fabric of this circular gang is the mysterious number Pi. You won't get far without encountering this Greek letter (π) and the many mathematical formulas that it finds its way into. Well, this well-rounded bunch completes our little math adventure—we've come full circle!

Circle

Circumference

Pi

Ellipse

Cylinder

Cone

Sphere

Circle
▪ In the Round

※ A perfectly round 2-D shape with a talent for rotating
※ Its edge stays an equal distance from its center point
※ You can draw this round, rolling wheel using a compass

Oh me, oh my, take a look at my ravishing, rotund lines. Unique in my roundness, I simply ooze perfection. I roll along without a care in the world. Life is *wheelie* good!

My largest width runs straight through my center and is called my diameter (*d*). My radius (*r*) is a straight line between my center and my edge—exactly half of my diameter. I'm deeply in love with Pi, who has a special relationship with Circumference (my perimeter). But you'll meet both of them later, so let's get back to me. I am the universe's most symmetrical two-dimensional shape, with an infinite number of lines of symmetry. Just think about it—every diameter you can draw is a line of reflectional symmetry! Spin me around my center and I look the same at all angles. Just perfect, wouldn't you agree?

● Diameter: $d = 2r$
● Area: $A = \pi r^2$
● The Olympic symbol is made up of five interlinked circles

Circle

111

Circumference

■ In the Round

* ✹ The perimeter, or edge, of a circle
* ✹ When the diameter of a circle is 1, its circumference is Pi (π)
* ✹ Provides largest area of any 2-D shape with same perimeter

Arise, Sir Cumference. I am a Knight of the Round and Able. Verily, I am the distance *around* the boundary of a perfectly circular object. Prithee roll with me, as I tell thee of my gallantry and dashing adventures!

My noble status comes from my link with Circle, the most perfect of all two-dimensional shapes. The borders of all other lowly forms belong to that peasant Perimeter. I run around wheels, toilet paper rolls, and jam jars. I can tell you the length a wheel will roll in one revolution and I'm used in odometers to calculate the distance traveled by a car or on your bike. I can even tell you how much cable will wrap around a cylindrical spool (should you ever need to know such a thing). Forsooth, there's no denying, I am an obliging old fellow!

* ● Circumference: $C = \pi d = 2\pi r$
* ● Arc: a portion of a circumference
* ● Chord: a straight line between two points on a circumference

Circumference

Pi

■ In the Round

✳ The ratio of a circle's circumference to its diameter: $C \div d$
✳ Denoted by the Greek letter π (say "pie")
✳ An irrational number that's been around for centuries

I'm a mathematical marvel, the most amazing number that there is! I'm the ratio of a circle's circumference to its diameter. No matter what size circle you have, this ratio is *always* the same. I help you find a circle's area and can solve countless other math problems.

Handle me at your peril, however, for I'm a mysterious Irrational Number. Infinitely complicated, my digits go on and on with no end. Currently, I am known to 27 trillion decimal places. As easy as π? That's as easy as 3.14159 26535 89793 23846 26433 83279 50288 41971 69399 37510 58209 74944 59230 78164 06286 20899 86280 34825 34211 70679 82148 08651 32823 . . . "How I wish I could calculate pi" gives you the first seven decimals if you count the number of letters in each word. Chew on that!

● World record for memorizing pi: Lu Chao (67,890 digits)
● Easy approximation for pi: $22 \div 7$
● Better approximation for pi: $355 \div 113$

Pi

Ellipse
■ In the Round

- ✳ A 2-D shape with a center and two focal points
- ✳ Has two axes running through its center
- ✳ Axes referred to as major axis (long) and minor axis (short)

A graceful oval, I bring a little glamour to the "In the Round" bunch. Imagine taking a horizontal slice through Cone—the cut end would be a circle. Now imagine taking a *slanting* slice and you get me—pretty Ellipse!

Here's a little exercise to help you understand me. Place a loop of string over two pins stuck into some thick cardboard. Draw around these pins, keeping within the loop of string and using your pencil to pull the loop taut as you go. Get back to where you started and there I am! The two pins mark my focal points, and the combined distance from both of these to any point on my perimeter is *always* a constant. Like Circle, I have a center. Planets use me as they swoop around the Sun. I have reflection symmetry around my axes and two-fold rotational symmetry.

- ● Half of each axis: semimajor axis (a) and semiminor axis (b)
- ● Area of an ellipse: $A = \pi a b$
- ● Major axis length of the Oval Office (U.S. president's office): 35.8 ft. (10.9m)

Ellipse

Cylinder
■ In the Round

✳ This high roller is known as a prism with a circular base
✳ A 3-D favorite for containing liquids
✳ Hollow versions get used as pipes and tunnels

Captain Cylinder rolling to the rescue! I am one of the most useful 3-D shapes that there is. My flat bottom is great for standing me upright on level ground. This is why you'll find me used as storage: soda cans, oil barrels, gas tanks, and rain barrels—you name it, I bottle it.

You can figure out my surface area by opening me out—I am made up of one rectangle wrapped around two circles (top and bottom). One side of the rectangle is simply my height. The other side is equal to the circumference of the circles or $2\pi r$. My total surface area is the area of the rectangle plus the area of both circles. As well as containers and hair rollers, my hollow shape forms all kinds of wheels to move you around. Once you get the hang of me, you'll be on a roll!

● Surface area of a cylinder's side: $2\pi rh$
● Surface area of a cylinder: $A = 2\pi rh + 2\pi r^2$
● Volume of a cylinder: $V = \pi r^2 h$

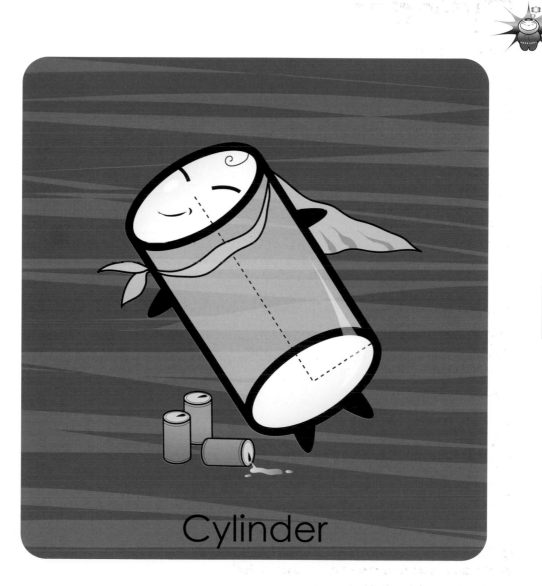

Cylinder

Cone

■ In the Round

✳ A 3-D shape that is a pyramid with a circular base
✳ Surfaces include a sector of one circle and one circle base
✳ Made by swiveling around a right triangle on its base

Put your hands together, kids! Everyone loves me! Why? Because great things come in my peculiar shape—treats like party hats and ice-cream cones—or traffic cones and wizard hats!

Call me a loose cannon if you want. I am a peculiar combination of a pyramid top with a circular bottom. Cut me from apex to base and you'll find my cross section makes two right triangles standing back to back. If you held one of these right triangles by its tip and spun it around on its 90° angle, you'd trace out my strange shape. My pointed end makes me ideal at the sharp end of drills, spears, and nails. You'll also find me perched at the end of your pencil after sharpening it. Now that's what I call wizardry!

● Volume of a cone: $V = \{1/3\}\pi r^2 h$
● Surface area of a cone: $S = \pi r[r + \sqrt{(r^2 + h^2)}]$
● Inventor of the traffic cone: Charles P. Rudebaker (1914)

Cone

Sphere
■ In the Round

✸ A perfectly round 3-D solid that is symmetrical in all directions
✸ A great shape for ball games
✸ Half a sphere is called a hemisphere

Content and placid, I'm a bouncing ball of fun. I have no points or sharp edges—I'm one real smooth dude. My uncanny ability to roll freely in any direction makes me the best shape for playing games. I'll keep you on your toes, forcing you to chase after me or training your hand–eye coordination to connect with a bat.

Spin a flat, two-dimensional circle, say a coin, around on any diameter and you will form my beautiful 3-D shape. I can be hollow inside—like a basketball—but my *shape* remains solid, because it fills 3-D space. Every point on my surface is an equal distance from my center. Earth and other planets are spheres, because the force of gravity attracts equally in all directions toward a central point. Outta this world!

● Volume of a sphere: $V = \frac{4}{3}\pi r^3$
● Surface area of a sphere: $A = 4\pi r^2$
● Number of tennis balls used at Wimbledon each year: around 50,000

Sphere

INDEX

Character entries are **bold**.

GLOSSARY

1-D Something with a single dimension (e.g., length); a line is one dimensional.

2-D Something with two dimensions (e.g., length and width); flat shapes are 2-D and have area.

3-D Something with three dimensions (e.g., length, width, and height); solid shapes are 3-D and have volume.

Arc Part of the circumference of a circle.

Axis (plural: **axes**) A fixed reference line for measuring coordinates on a graph.

Constant A value in an equation that is not a variable (that is, it doesn't change: in $y = x - 5$, 5 is the constant).

Cubic Any equation or mathematical relationship where the maximum value index of the variables is 3 (cube).

Decimal place The position of a number to the right of a decimal point.

Denominator The bottom part of a fraction; stands for the total number of equal parts in a fraction.

Diameter A straight line from edge to edge on a circle, drawn through the center; twice the radius.

Divisor A number that divides into another.

Exterior angle The angle made between the outer edge of a 2-D shape and the extension of the side next to it.

Focal point A fixed point, where the distances from it to any point on a curve or shape are related in a simple way (e.g., are always a constant); also called focus.

Formula A mathematical rule that is written algebraically.

Index (plural: **indices**) A small number written to the right and above a number, which tells you how many of the larger number should be multiplied together; also known as an exponent.

Infinity A number bigger than any imaginable number.

Interior angle Any of the angles inside a polygon.

Intersect When two lines (1-D), planes (2-D), or surfaces (3-D) meet, cross, or pass through each other.

Limit A value that an equation or a function approaches.

Linear An equation or any mathematical relationship where the variables are not raised by an exponent (the index is 1); a linear function always gives a straight-line graph.

Magnitude The size of a vector, found by forming a right triangle with its x and y components.

Natural number The whole, positive numbers that you use to count things.

Numerator The top part of a fraction; the number of pieces being considered as part of a whole.

Parallel When lines (1-D), planes (2-D), or surfaces (3-D) keep the same distance from each other, never touching.

Perpendicular When lines (1-D), planes (2-D), or surfaces (3-D) intersect at right angles.

GLOSSARY

Place value The value of a digit, depending on its position (e.g., the position of the number 2 in 20 and 200 assigns each figure with a different value).

Prime factor A factor of a composite number that is a prime number.

Prism A 3-D, solid shape whose two ends are exactly the same and parallel and whose side edges are parallel.

Quadratic Any equation or mathematical relationship where the maximum value index of the variables is 2 (square).

Radius A straight line from the center of a circle to its edge; half the diameter.

Ratio A way of comparing two numbers; can be written as a fraction, as the first number over the second.

Real number Any number that is not imaginary.

Remainder The amount left over when one number isn't divided exactly by another.

Right angle A 90° angle.

Scale factor The value by which a shape is enlarged or reduced.

Set (as in set of all . . .) A group of numbers that all have something in common.

Variable An unknown number in an equation or function.

Vertex (plural: **vertices**) The place where two sides of a 2-D shape, or three or more faces of a 3-D shape, meet; a corner.